# SCREAMING FROM THE INSIDE

## OVERCOMING MOLESTATION AND SEXUAL ABUSE

# SCREAMING FROM THE INSIDE

## Overcoming Molestation and Sexual Abuse

Kmetris Hunt

XULON PRESS

Xulon Press
2301 Lucien Way #415
Maitland, FL 32751
407.339.4217
www.xulonpress.com

ISBN-13: 978-1-5456-7128-3

# TABLE OF CONTENTS

# ACKNOWLEDGMENTS

*Proverbs 3:5-6 "Trust in the LORD with all thine heart; and lean not unto thine own understanding. In all thy ways acknowledge him, and he shall direct thy paths."*

I give all glory, honor and thanks unto my Abba Father who I literally had to trust, lean on, acknowledge and get direction from in order to fulfill this mandate He placed on me. It is because of HIM and the Holy Spirit that has enabled me through this process.

I want to thank my husband, Will Hunt for being by my side every step of the way through this journey. You have been my greatest supporter and strength. When I wanted to give up, you encouraged me to keep going. You have seen me experience every emotion through this journey.

I would also like to thank ALL my children, especially the 4 I birthed out of my womb (Darrell, Katrise, Demetri and Kayla) for their encouragement in coming forth with my story.

I want to especially thank my book mentor, Dr. Trina Wells, Certified Life Coach, Author and Inspirational

Speaker, for your unwavering support. If it had not been for God strategically placing you in my life, I would not have written this book. I thank you for affording me the opportunity to be a part of 2 of your book collaborations to prepare me for this journey. Thank you for answering my calls, texts, encouraging me in every phase and not letting me give up. Thank you for your prayers and being a strength.

I would also like to thank my dearest friends, (Stephanie, Terri, Tahesha, Veronica, Amber and Ron) who listened to me, saw and heard me weep, yet you continued to stick by my side and pushed me with many encouraging words and prayers.

Lastly, I dedicate this book to every individual, male or female that has experienced any form of abuse. My continual prayers are with you for your healing.

# IT
# IS
# NOT
# YOUR
# FAULT

# FOREWORD

## *(A conversation with the reader)*

This is my first book on my own, however I am grateful for the opportunity to have written in 2 book collaborations beforehand to get acclimated with writing my story. I was inspired to write this book in 12 parts depicting the process to completion. The number 12 represents divine power, governmental authority and completeness. This book is my personal journey to how I received my healing by walking in and executing the divine power and authority God has given me. Prayerfully my story will help someone else in their process of healing of any form of abuse whether sexual, physical, mental or emotional.

First and foremost, I would like to say to every person, whether male or female, who has been a victim of sexual or physical abuse, *"IT IS NOT YOUR FAULT!"* There is absolutely nothing you have done or could ever do to make someone violate you in such a traumatic way. It does not matter the situation, no one has the right to take advantage of you, force themselves *upon you nor physically harm you. For those of you who have never experienced sexual abuse,*

*my prayer is that you will get a better understanding of those who have.*

*What I have discovered over the years dealing with my own abuse, is that there are those who tend to blame the victim for the violations that have happened to them. For some reason, it is assumed that YOU, the victim had to have done something to bring the abuse upon yourself. This is furthest from the truth! I have heard and/or read where many people make statements like, "You must have wanted it!" or "She was fast!" It is such statements and labels like this that keep girls/women and boys/men from speaking up about what they have been through. Why would we tell anyone what we have suffered through, just to be blamed? Why would we open up ourselves and share our secrets, for no one to believe us? Have you ever wondered maybe the reason she is fast is because she has been touched prematurely? Those of us that have had any experience with sex know once you get a taste of it, you tend to want more. However, in the cases of molestation and sexual abuse "SEX" has been perverted and twisted so, that it leaves the victim mentally unstable. So imagine being a little girl that was touched too soon and now she is in her teens wanting the attention of boys and men. She does not even understand why she wants the attention. She does not even understand why she has a desire for sex, when in all actuality sex is not what she is even looking for. What she is really looking for is love, but her love has been tainted and perverted and now she thinks sex is love.*

*I have learned that if you have not experienced it, there is a possibility that you may not understand it. I generally do not speak on things I am not familiar with or have not experienced. If someone shares their experiences with me, I at least try to put myself in their shoes and get an understanding of what they have been through. Most critics do not look to get an understanding, they just look to be right or point the finger! Proverbs 4:7 says, "Wisdom is the principle thing; therefore get wisdom: and with all thy getting (of wisdom) get understanding.*

*In cases when it comes to sexual or even physical abuse, things are not always black and white. There are a few factors to be considered when it comes to the circumstances surrounding the abuse that are often overlooked.*

*The main question most people ask victims after waiting years to speak out about it is:*

**Why did you wait so long to tell someone? Well let me answer that for you...**
*The main reason why victims do not tell, is FEAR! From my experience, fear has played the major role in me not sharing what happened to me. The victim is usually being threatened not to tell or something bad will happen to them or their family. There is usually some*

form of manipulation involved as well to keep the victim from speaking out. The abuser may use fear tactics to hold things over the victims head to keep them from revealing their secret. There is also the fear of family members and friends not believing you. Somehow in a warped way, we have convinced ourselves that this has to be our fault, and no one will believe us. The other thing to consider is if it is in fact a family member that victimized you. If that is the case, you will fear getting them in trouble. WHY? Because you love them outside of the abuse!!! FEAR is a monster and will paralyze you and keep you from seeking help. THERE IS NO TIMELINE ON FEAR!!!

For me, all I knew is that I did not want to suffer anymore. It came to a point where I just had to choose me over it. And guess what? Fear was present then as well! I just wanted out of the situation. I had gotten to the point where I was old enough to try to do something about it. It was going to take a plan of action and a lot of courage. But what happens when you finally break free, you tell your secret, but no one believes you or helps you? What happens when your abuser takes a lie detector test, passes it and the powers that be send you right back home to your abuser? What happens when you have no evidence to prove what has happened to you? What happens when it is the victim's word over the abuser's word?

## Part 1

## INTRODUCTION

## Child Molestation and Sexual Abuse Statistics

### 'Look Closer'

Child molesters and or sexual predators come from all economic backgrounds, geographic areas including every ethnicity, race and creed. You can not judge a book by its cover; therefore, it is not based off a certain look.

WHAT IS A CHILD MOLESTER?

Someone who has the thought about being sexual with children then go about seeking access and alone time with them. Child molesters are usually someone close to you like a family member, whether a parent, step-parent, grandparent, sibling, uncle, aunt or cousin. Statistics states that the percentage of child sexual abuse committed by a family member is:

- 49% of victims under age of 6
- 42% of victims ages 7-11
- 24% of victims ages 12-17

It can also be a friend of the family or babysitter, generally someone who spends a lot of time around the family. According to invisiblechildren.org, 90% of child sexual abuse victims know their predators. This means that the chances of you being sexually abused by a stranger is 10%.

I am reminded of a story in the bible about a virgin named Tamar. Tamar had a half-brother named Amnon who was highly attracted to her. He was so infatuated with her that he devised a plan to sleep with her. He pretended to be ill and asked his father if Tamar could fix him some food and bring it to him to eat from her hand. The father agreed. When Tamar came into the room with the food, Amnon preceded to make advances at her. When she refused her brother, he raped her. After the rape, Amnon no longer loved his half-sister. Amnon saw what he wanted, sought her out and preyed upon her. Tamar was raped by someone she loved and trusted. He was not a stranger!

The molester preys on its victim by befriending and grooming them over a period of time. Befriending and grooming of its victim consists of being extra nice, giving special privileges or making the child feel special and the giving of gifts or money. This makes the child more comfortable and vulnerable with the molester.

These tactics can also be used on online social media platforms such as Facebook, etc.

It is very important for parents to closely monitor their children as molesters often seek alone time with their victims. If you are a parent who does not pay close attention to your child or your child's whereabouts; then your child becomes easy prey for the molester. Trust me, the molester sees and knows that you may not give your child enough attention and therefore will seek to access your child by befriending them with positive attention. You must periodically ask your child if anyone as touched them or tried to violate them in any way. Also, watch your child's behavior and mood swings as they will show some sign of molestation like; uneasiness around the molester, wetting the bed, never wanting to go over a particular persons house, etc. And PARENTS, if your child comes to you and tell you someone has violated them, please take the time to listen and believe them. So many times children are subjected to ongoing abuse because no one believed them. If they tell you, it is imperative to at least investigate.

# Reflection Journal

What does an abuser look like to you?

_____

_____

_____

_____

_____

_____

_____

_____

_____

_____

_____

_____

_____

_____

_____

# THE STORY

# Part 2

## HAPPY DAYS

I was about five or six years old living in a small town in Mississippi. Most of my time was spent with my grandmother who had me spoiled rotten, but she did not play no games. On the weekends we would always go to town with my favorite aunt and cousin. "TOWN" is where you go to do your shopping and literally hang out for the day. It was like a mini field trip in my mind and full of fun. We would always come back home with something, whether a piece of clothing or a toy. I remember us always going to McDonald's at the end of the day to get our happy meal. There was this one time my cousin and I begged for a big mac. Mind you, we were only five years of age, so my grandmother and aunt thought a big mac would absolutely be too much to eat, but on this particular day, they bought it for us. I remember stuffing myself trying to force it down my throat until I just could not eat anymore. As they had predicted, it was indeed too much for a five-year old.

When I would go to my aunt's house, which was often; there were days we would go berry and pecan picking. My aunt lived on a farm and raised cattle, chickens and pigs. I would often feed the animals which was fun at that time. She also had a garden where we would help her plant seeds for vegetables and fruits. We enjoyed the simple things in life like, running up and down the rock road bare feet, playing hide and seek, playing jump rope, chasing frogs and lightning bugs. These were some of the best days of my life.

My grandmother soon passed away and I was devastated. She had poured so much into me as a child. One of my fondest memories is of her teaching me the Lord's Prayer and we would say it together every night before bedtime and it has been my tradition ever since.

Soon after grandmother's passing, we began making our journey through several states and cities before finally settling in Chicago. Moving to Chicago was the beginning and ending of who I was and what I had known my life to be.

# **Reflection Journal**

Recall some happy days when you were a child.

_____

_____

_____

_____

_____

_____

_____

_____

_____

_____

_____

_____

_____

_____

_____

_____

_____

# Part 3

## THE PREY AND THE ABUSE

Living in Chicago was definitely different from the small town in Mississippi. Everything in Chicago was bigger and brighter, as we did not have many street lights in the south which means you needed to be in the house before dark and before the mosquitos came out. But here in Chicago, we could stay out later seeing as we had lights to see. I'm about nine years old now and still happy enjoying spending time with more family. I remember attending a lot of family functions and cook-outs at this time in my life. At some point, at the age of ten, I had an encounter with someone who had become very close with my family. This individual began taking a liking to my mother and they soon became a couple. He was very kind and gave me special attention and would always offer me candy or money and plenty of compliments. Naturally, as a young girl whose father was not present in her life, I took a liking to this man. Nothing in me sounded an alarm that it could turn into anything other than him being nice to me. I trusted him!

It all began with what appeared to be a teaching lesson on sexual intercourse. It seemed innocent at first.

He would talk to me about sex and then preceded to show me his penis. Then it went from him showing it to me to him rubbing it on me and having me touch it. I began to feel uncomfortable and did not like it. I knew this wasn't right and I remember trying to pull away saying "NO" to him. He would stop and would tell me that it was okay and to not tell anyone and that if I told, he would hurt me. Naturally, I was afraid to say anything, so I didn't. Well, because I was so afraid to say anything, these episodes continued happening and grew worse. He became forceful, would not stop or take no for an answer. I wanted to scream for help, but he would cover my mouth and threaten me not to tell anyone. It went from fondling my vagina with his hands and penis on to full blown penetration. After each time, he would always remind me not tell anyone or he would hurt me or my family. Then it went from just hurting me to killing me.

It was at this moment that I realized my life had turned for the worst. The child I once was, no longer existed. I was no longer happy and became very angry. I hated my abuser and wanted to kill him. There were times I would plot in my mind on how I could get rid of him. He would often send me for his water or some other beverage. The thoughts often came to put some type of poison in his drink. I hated being around him and wanted him gone. I did not trust anyone and began to dislike people altogether. Most times, my abuse would happen in the middle of the night when everyone else was asleep. I always knew when it was going to happen because the drinking of alcohol would often play a factor. This was usually after some type of gathering at the house or after an argument. I would try to pretend that I was asleep so he would go away, but he would not take no for an answer. I would be threatened if I did not get up. The strange thing is that we always had someone living with us, but never did anyone get up in the middle of the night to check on things. Had someone did, I may have been saved from the abuse. There were also times I was taken away from the house as if we were going on a trip to the store or something and he would have sex with me. I have even experienced being secretly fondled while in the car right under the noses of a family member or even during family get togethers. I would try to find ways to get out of the house, but I was never allowed to go anywhere. Then there was the physical abuse that began along with the sexual abuse to make sure I would never tell. He was a very angry man and often took out his anger on others. So, if I had done anything wrong around the house or at school, I could expect a beating. It did not matter how great or small the incident, I would be beaten until I was bleeding and was threatened repeatedly. I would wear long sleeve sweaters to hide the scars whenever I went to school or out in public. I would also spend weeks on punishment for the smallest things I would do. I was told I would be killed and so would others in my family. It wasn't as much about me saving my life that I did not tell, but I did not want to see anyone else I loved, lose their life. Constantly afraid, I had become enclosed into this box of abuse that no one else knew about. This had gone on for four years straight, and it was my horrible secret. I became insecure about myself and my body. There was nothing wrong with my body, but in my mind whatever it was that was bringing on what was happening to me, I did not want it to be exposed. That said, I began to wear long sleeve button down sweaters to cover my skin. It would be summertime and I would have a sweater on with shorts and sandals. I began to pull back from people and trusted no one from this point on. I was no longer me, I was someone else.

This was the enemies plan. John 10:10 says, *"the thief (the devil) cometh not, but for to steal, and to kill, and to destroy: I (Jesus) am come that they might have life, and that they might have it more abundantly."* The enemy began stealing from my life, piece by piece. The joy that I once had, began to diminish. Yes, I would still have moments of laughter, but there was no real happiness or joy. I began to feel numb and lifeless on the inside. Yet, I acted as if everything was normal as I continued to hold in my secret from day to day.

# **Reflection Journal**

If you were abused, Journal your experience...

_____

_____

_____

_____

_____

_____

_____

_____

_____

_____

_____

_____

_____

_____

_____

_____

# Part 4

## THE COVER UP
## SCREAMING FROM THE INSIDE

I remember going day in and day out with my secret.
I often say, there is a thin line between secrecy and
privacy. Now there are some good harmless secrets like
a surprise birthday party, but then there are those secrets
that destroy us from the inside out. I had a secret that
was literally killing me on the inside, and I needed to tell
someone. I had a secret that was threatening my life, but
I did not know how to tell it. My secret was making me
sick because I could not find the strength to release it.
I was "SCREAMING FROM THE INSIDE!" I needed
help, but no one could hear me. Yet, I continued to put
up this façade in the presence of those I came in con-
tact with day after day. I had to pretend that everything
was okay. I continued to interact normally at school
and around family members. I was good at smiling and
laughing through the pain, yet I was "SCREAMING
FROM THE INSIDE!" I hoped someone could hear
me. I wished someone could see what was happening
to me or at least sense it. That is why until this day, I
am very sensitive to the effects of child molestation and

abuse. I often find myself assessing children when they are around me. I can sometimes even sense a sexual predator when in my presence. I would wonder how many young girls and boys, I passed by each day, were holding secrets of sexual molestation or physical abuse. I even wonder how many adult men and women are covering up a secret that they have been dealing with since they were a child. One thing I learned about covering things up is that it does not go away just because it is covered. Even though no one could see it, I still had to sit in it and deal with it.

I was literally "SCREAMING FROM THE INSIDE" trying to figure out how to tell someone. Even though I could not speak out loud about it, the evidence was there. The emotional scars were there. The sadness I felt was there. The mental anguish was there. All of these things began to manifest within me and then came out in anger and bitterness. There were those who thought I was just a typical teenager with an attitude problem, but it was far beyond that. I needed help, but no one could hear my cry from the inside. At this point, I was 14 and felt I had enough strength to come forth with my secret, but who could I tell. Whenever you are in an abusive situation, who you tell could mean life or death. It had to be someone I could trust and that I knew without a doubt, would help me. Unfortunately for me, I really did not feel like I had anyone that fit in that category. First all, who would believe me? Then it was the factor of me not wanting to get anyone else in trouble.

This was a lot of pressure for a young teenage girl to be under. I debated back and forth within myself on how to get out and tell someone. I would rehearse my plan over and over again in my mind. I thought about how I could sneak out of the house in the middle of the night and runaway. However, I was very afraid of being caught. It was going to take a lot of courage to pull this off. So, I told myself that I was going to leave the next time the abuse happens. But the day would soon come where my inside screams turned into outside screams.

# **Reflection Journal**

Are you covering up anything that is destroying you on the inside?

_____

_____

_____

_____

_____

_____

_____

_____

_____

_____

_____

_____

_____

_____

# Part 5

## THE GREAT ESCAPE

O ne night after my abuser's much drinking, I ended up being not only raped, but beaten as well. I'm not sure what I had done to be beaten that night, but it was done in anger and rage. I had been beaten to the point of bleeding all over my body. I remember saying to myself, "This is it!" I couldn't take it anymore. So as everyone slept, I snuck out of the house and ran as fast as I could to the nearest police station. I did it! I finally did it! I escaped my abuser. I told the police officer what happened and showed them the scars on my body and they immediately took me to the hospital.

While at the hospital, they began to examine my body and run all types of tests on me. I found out that my blood vessels had been broken because of the severe beating. The next morning, I met with a social worker from the Department of Children and Family Services. I told them what I been through and they sent me to a girls group home. While there, the police had brought my abuser in for questioning. I was told they gave him a lie detector test, that he somehow passed and they sent him back home.

I am now living in a group home with other troubled teenage girls. Although this place was better than being at home, it still had its bad moments. I did not like it there and wanted to go home, but not back to the abusive situation. I felt so alone and cried a lot. After being there for about a week, my social worker asked me if I wanted to go back home. She told me that my abuser had been asked to leave the home and that it was safe for me to go back if I wanted to. I felt relieved to know I could go back home and was very happy. However, there was an unexpected surprise waiting for me when I came through the door.

## *Note*

*If you are still in an abusive situation, it is imperative that you seek help. You must come up with a strategic plan for your escape.*

Nationwide abuse hotline #'s
Child Abuse Hotline: 800.25.ABUSE
Sexual Assault Hotline: 800.656.
HOPE (4673)

# **Reflection Journal**

Journal your escape plan...

_____

_____

_____

_____

_____

_____

_____

_____

_____

_____

_____

_____

_____

_____

_____

_____

# Part 6

## DEATH CAME KNOCKING

As I walked through the door after returning home from being in the custody of DCFS, I was met by my abuser. He began to remind me of the promise he made if I ever told what he had been doing to me all those years and was about to make good on his promise. As family members stood around screaming and yelling, he preceded to go and get his gun. He put the gun to the temple of my head and said, "Didn't I tell you I would kill you if you ever told?" At this point in my life (14 years old), I was no longer afraid of the threats. I was tired and didn't want to live anyway. I had had enough and didn't want to suffer anymore. I had made up in my mind that I was not taking the abuse anymore, therefore I did not care. My secret was finally out, and I just wanted to be free, even if it meant death. This situation had taken its toll on me and I had nothing to fight for at this point. It's amazing to me how life didn't matter to me. I was willing to let it all end right there in that moment. I had no fear of death. I was not afraid anymore.

So, I am standing there without a care in world thinking to myself, if this is living, I do not want to live. Then I said to him, "Shoot me!" There were family members yelling and screaming at him telling him no and to put the gun down. One family member in particular challenged my abuser, which caused an altercation between the two of them. This then took the attention off me and my abuser turned the gun and pointed it toward the family member. They began to wrestle with one another, but the family member could not get the gun from him. My abuser threatened to kill the family and the family member ran to the nearest window and jumped out. Somehow the commotion came to an end and things went back to normal. We were required to go through several sessions of counseling after the incident, which did not help if you ask me.

I am now preparing and focusing on graduating from elementary school. Soon thereafter we moved into a smaller apartment, which afforded me an opportunity to go and stay with one of my aunts back home in Mississippi. But how is it that the very thing you try to run from, you end up running right back into it? I thought I had gotten away from everything I had been through, but abuse sure had a way of finding ME.

## **Reflection Journal**

During your experience, were you ever at the point of death?

_____

_____

_____

_____

_____

_____

_____

_____

_____

_____

_____

_____

_____

_____

# Part 7

## NO ESCAPING

It is summertime in Mississippi and I am having the best time of my life. Finally feeling some relief from everything I have been through. I am meeting new friends and preparing for my freshman year of high school. I am excited about this new venture in my life. School begins, and I instantly join the track and field team. I absolutely loved running and I won several medals and trophies while in elementary and high school. Running was an outlet for me when I was feeling abandoned and alone. I was a part of something that I could call family and I enjoyed it.

Finally, I can enjoy my life without worrying about someone coming into my room at night to harm me. Well that was until one night when I stayed at one of my family member's house for a sleep over. During the night, her husband came in the room where I was laying and began touching me inappropriately. I manage to fight him off and I am not sure how many days it took me, but I went and told my cousin. She believed me and addressed it. I am not exactly sure what happened, but he ended up no longer being a part of our family.

So now I am thinking to myself, am I ever going to get away from people like this? Why do these grown men go around touching on young girls? These men have wives of their own and children. Then I began to wonder to myself if there was something about me that was inviting this type of behavior into my life. But I knew I didn't do anything to bring this on. This was not something I wanted to happen. These men have serious problems and issues that at the time I did not totally understand.

So we get past that, school is going well and then I meet a guy my age. We began to hang out, eventually became intimate and I ended up pregnant towards the end of my freshman school year. After my pregnancy was found out, my mom came to get me and brought me back to Chicago. There was no way I could continue to stay with my aunt after getting pregnant. She could not take care of me and a baby! And of course, I did not want to leave my baby's father, but I had no choice. I was only 16 and had no clue about raising a child. This was the beginning of another phase of my life.

# **Reflection Journal**

Have you ever tried to escape an abusive situation, but couldn't?

_____

_____

_____

_____

_____

_____

_____

_____

_____

_____

_____

_____

_____

_____

## Part 8

# LOOKING FOR LOVE IN ALL THE WRONG PLACES

So I am back at home again and pregnant with my son. Me and my son's father tried to maintain a long-distance relationship, but we couldn't manage to make it work. I had to register into an alternative school for pregnant teens for my sophomore year of high school, which was the best option for me considering my situation. I was afforded some opportunities through going to this particular school which prepared me to move forward with my baby. There was this one teacher I will never forget. Her name was Ms. Strickland and she taught typing and professional development. She took me under her wing while I was there and walked me through some really rough times. I was a really good student and did well at typing, therefore she took a liking to me. I got my very first job because of her. She literally prepared me for the interview, told me what to wear and drove me there. She introduced me to the manager and spoke very highly of me and he gave me the job.

During this time, I was still struggling with my own inner issues and insecurities due to my abuse. All I really wanted was to be loved my someone. I had become very sexually active and ended up pregnant again by another guy. Sex was all I really knew seeing as I was introduced to it at such a young age. So I figured if I had sex with a guy he would eventually love me. Well, I did not need or want another child at this point in my life. How was I going to take care of another child? I was barely taking care of the one I had. I began to beat myself up about getting pregnant again. I was ashamed. I felt I just could not get my life together. I was emotionally broken and scarred looking to be fixed. Having another child was not going to fix me, therefore I ended up getting an abortion. That was one of the worst experiences of my life. The mental toll it took on me and let's not even mention the amount of guilt I had to endure because of my choice. But it did not stop there!

Shortly after, I came across a former crush from grammar school and we became a couple. I had known him to be a sweet person back in grammar school, but had no idea what type of person he had become. As time went on, I eventually moved in with him and his family. Mind you, I am only 17 years old, but I was seeking for some type of relief. However, I just ran from one abusive situation into another. Shortly after moving in, my boyfriend became very possessive and abusive toward me. I remember us walking to school together one time; he picked up a big 2 x 4 piece of wood and began beating me with it. There was also a time at school when he got so jealous over me talking to another guy that he grabbed me by my neck, slammed me against the locker and choked me. Then preceded to say these words to me, "If I can't have you no one else will."

At one point I thought it was flattering and meant that he loved me. Because I had seen abuse and experienced abuse so much this had to mean he loved me and did not want to lose me. So naturally I stayed with him and tolerated the abuse. But then it began to get worse to the point of my life being in danger.

One day on our way home from school, we had an altercation. During the alteration he told me he was going to kill me if I try to leave him. I tried to fight him off and walk away. He then preceded to throw my body in front of a moving vehicle. The car stopped before hitting me. He then rammed my head into a brick wall. I somehow got away from him and never went back to him after that. Once I saw him in a Walgreens, and I ran and hid so he wouldn't see me. That was the last time seeing him. Thank GOD!!!

Now, I am in my senior year of high school. I met another guy who was 4 years older than I was. Once again, here I am looking for love in all the wrong places. I was trying to fulfill a void in my life that these men nor sex could fill. I did not know what real love from a man looked or felt like. The love I was looking for was the love of my father. Unfortunately, my father was not in my life growing up, therefore I did not receive the proper love and attention I needed. Not only that, but I was not able to identify "love" because I had never been taught. But LOVE would soon find me.

# **Reflection Journal**

In what areas of your life have you looked for love or validation?

_____

_____

_____

_____

_____

_____

_____

_____

_____

_____

_____

_____

_____

_____

# THE HEALING

# Part 9

## IDENTITY CRISIS: YOU ARE NOT WHAT HAPPENED TO YOU

Have you ever wondered what type of person you would have been if you had not gone through some of the tragedies in your life? The wonderful thing about it is that even though we may not know why certain things have occurred in our lives, God knows why and has a purpose and plan for it. In Jeremiah 29:11, God says to us, *"For I know the plans I have for you, declares the Lord, plans to prosper you and not harm you, plans to give you hope and a future."* For myself, not realizing at the time what God had in store for me, I allowed those experiences to cause me to become someone who God had not created me to be. It had shaped me into a person whose life was filled with pain and anger that manifested itself on a regular basis.

In life we will experience some things that will affect us positively and or negatively. These experiences usually dictate the type of influence it will have on our future self. Because of the many years of abuse, heartache and pain I had endured, I became someone I did not even recognize or like. I had allowed what had happened to me to enter into my heart, thereby becoming bitter and cold. I would lash out at others because of my own pain and I had become one with it. I was like the woman in the bible who had a spirit of infirmity for 18 years. (Luke 13:11). The bible says she was bent over and could not come out of the state or position she was in. She had been influenced and paralyzed by her circumstance to the point where she could not pull herself up out of her dilemma. That was me!!!

# **Reflection Journal**

Did your experience cause you to have self-identity issues?

_____

_____

_____

_____

_____

_____

_____

_____

_____

_____

_____

_____

_____

_____

# Part 10

## LOVE HAD A PLAN

The bible lets us know in John 3:16 that God loved us so, that He gave His only son for us. Well I did not recognize this kind of love because I wasn't familiar with someone sacrificing their life for me. So here I am now at the age of 18 and after having my second child, God sends a young lady to minister to me. I remember working at a store and she worked in the jewelry department which was located right by the front door as you walked in. Every day when I walked through the door, she would approach me to invite me to her church. She would persistently tell me how much Jesus loved me and that He wanted to save me.

I would think to myself, "Jesus can't possibly love me." I tried ignoring her but that didn't stop her from reaching out to me every single time she saw me. I would wear a baseball cap in order to hide my face so she wouldn't notice me when I came through the door. Needless to say, that did not work either. After much compelling, I finally gave in and decided to go with her. See, God knew what I needed, when I needed it and who to send to speak into my life. It was a Friday night service; a night I will never forget. I gave my life to the Lord and was filled with the Holy Spirit that night. God's presence was all over me and I couldn't seem to stop it. I kneeled in prayer longing and desiring for more of him and that feeling of love.

Even after that, I yet had to deal with my demons of abuse. And because no one was teaching me or showing me how to get healed, I kept falling into traps of manipulation and abuse. Even after I had given my life to Christ, I was still being preyed upon in the church house. It seemed as if I had a sign on my forehead that read, "OPEN FOR ABUSE!" I eventually got married at age 19 so I wouldn't go to hell, as they kept telling me I would. Once again, I am in a situation where the love ain't right, but it is better than what I had experienced. I was so dysfunctional that I thought certain things were normal based off my experiences. And because of that mindset, I continued to stay in situations with wrong people for far too long. I would leave home being told I wasn't good enough to going to church being told I wasn't good enough, that I had pride, that I was rebellious and many other things. I was taught not to speak up for myself, because when I did, it was pride. No one seemed to like me when I spoke up for myself. I was taught to just follow leadership and not think on my own. And that is just what I did, thereby becoming someone other than myself. I had lost me!

I then began to seek for fulfillment outside of my marriage because I still was not happy. When you don't know what love is, there is no way you can maintain healthy and whole relationships with others. When I finally came to my senses, I got a divorce and left some other situations that were not healthy for me. Afterwards, I remember being so thin because I had no appetite to eat because of depression. But even through all of that, I still wanted God so bad. I wanted to know Him and feel His presence after being ostracized and abandoned by so many. When it was all said and done, it was just me and God. I had no one else to lean on nor call on at this point. I didn't want to give of myself to anyone, and I didn't want anyone trying to love me.

But one day, as I fell down on my knees in the middle of my living room floor, I began to cry out to God for help. After being labeled and told I wasn't chosen, all I could do was weep before God. There's a phrase we often used as kids that says, "Sticks and stones may break my bones, but words will never hurt me." Well, that isn't true...words do hurt and can also have an effect on you mentally depending on what is said and who is saying it. However, God began to tell me His thoughts towards me, which were of peace and not of evil to give me an expected end (Jer. 29:11). He told me how much He loves me and how He wanted me and that I had put my trust in people, more than in Him. He had chosen me, and no one could take that from me. When I heard that, I began to rejoice and picked myself up off the floor. It is God who validates us, not man, but I still needed to do the work.

# **Reflection Journal**

Did anyone come into your life to help jump start your journey to healing?

_____

_____

_____

_____

_____

_____

_____

_____

_____

_____

_____

_____

_____

_____

# Part 11

## FORGIVENESS HEALED ME

After many years of struggling, divorced, depressed and in what seems like a backslidden state, I began to hear the voices in my head telling me to kill myself. I remember falling on my face again before God asking him to help me. God answered my prayer by sending a man of God and his wife my way to show me what real love looks like. I remember telling him my story and then asking him if he was going to kick me to the curb like all the others. He looked at me in my eyes and said, "No daughter!", then proceeded to hug me tightly as I cried. That was a turning point moment in my life where I sincerely felt loved. Now do not get me wrong, I am sure there were others who loved me, but the feeling had been deadened. One Sunday during the morning service, the man of God was praying for me and told me the Lord was bringing me to a place of healing. He began to speak in my life all of the things God had planned for me and told me that I was going to move on to do the will of God for my life.

From that moment on I committed myself to going down to the church every morning before work to pray.

Not long after that, my now husband came into my life and he took me to hear his uncle preach. The man of God preached a word on forgiveness that changed my life forever. Granted, I thought I had forgiven some people, but after hearing his message, I realized I had not. I literally cried through the whole entire message. I can still hear those words today saying, *"Unforgiveness is like drinking poison, but expecting the other person to die."* In my mind, I thought I was hurting the other person, not knowing I was only hurting myself.

The process of healing began when I first chose to love and forgive myself for all of the dumb mistakes, shame and self-disappointment. My road to healing was not an easy task. It took me coming face to face with what had happened to me. For years I did not want to face it; I would rather just bury it and be angry about it. I also had to acknowledge the fact that I needed healing and that I could no longer hide from my scars. The longer I held on to it, the more it damaged me inwardly and my relationships with others. I did not trust, therefore kept a lot of people at a distance. And even if I did open up, I was always skeptical of the person. But now I had finally gotten to the point where I wanted to let it go for good.

Then I called out every person's name in prayer that I had not forgiven. In Matthew 6, Jesus said, *"For if you forgive other people when they sin against you, your heavenly Father will also forgive you."* With that, the chains began to fall away, my eyes of understanding were enlightened, and my heart was open to give and receive love again. Through this process, God granted my desire to minister to many hurting young girls and women, which brought salvation, healing and restoration to their lives.

## **<u>Note to the reader:</u>**

Healing is vital to your growth! It is imperative that you first acknowledge your pain and that you need healing. Then you must forgive yourself and those who have taken advantage of you in any shape, form or fashion in order to receive your complete and total healing. It is not easy, but you can do it with God's strength. When we continue to hold on to our hurts, pains and dysfunctions, we then become unrelatable to people. Holding on affects every part of your lives, within and without. My prayer is that God will give you the strength to

LET IT GO TODAY AND BE HEALED!!!

# **Reflection Journal**

Continue to journal your healing process...

_____

_____

_____

_____

_____

_____

_____

_____

_____

_____

_____

_____

_____

_____

_____

_____

# THE OVERCOMER

## Part 12

# LET 'YOU' ARISE-REFUSE TO BE A VICTIM

'LET' – Hebrew (Phonetic: haw-yaw) To Be, Become and ARISE.

*Too often we live by and or cater to the perceptions, ideas and standards of others rather than those which were predestined by God from the beginning.*

> *"You can't do that!"*
> *"You can't go there!"*
> *"You can't have that!"*

*We will sometimes allow ourselves to be manipulated by others into putting our own desires and plans on the shelf while pushing their visons and desires forward. We have even allowed our circumstances and dilemmas to shape us into someone other than what we were created to be...so much to the point that we don't really know who we are.*

*Just think about the time someone asked you, "Who are you?" Nine times out of ten, you couldn't tell them who you were. WHY?? Because what WE think of or know about ourselves is usually out of reach and the only way to respond is to rehearse what others have already told us about ourselves.*

*There is a greater and better you that awaits! A YOU, that you have never seen or known. A YOU, you must face in order to overcome!*

*As often quoted by Poet, Marianne Williamson:*
*"Our deepest fear is not that we are inadequate.*
*Our deepest fear is that we are powerful beyond measure."*

Jeremiah 2:21 says, *"Yet I had planted thee a noble vine, wholly a right seed: how then art thou turned into the degenerate plant of a strange **vine** unto me?"* See, when God planted us, He created us noble and whole. We were honorable in our own right, stablished, and true to ourselves. We were created without dysfunction, however because of the fall of man, we were shaped into iniquity and conceived into sin; thereby causing us to sometimes not live the abundant life set before us. Though I suffered and been through the valley of darkness, my light finally came.

Now that I know who I am in HIM, I have no choice but to be WHOLE!

*Everything that sought to take me out, DID'NT!*
*Everything the enemy threw my way to destroy me, COULDN'T!*

*WHY?*

*Because GOD has the final say so concerning my life! His word was already settled in heaven for me. His promise is sure!*

*I chose to use what I had been through for HIS GLORY and to help others.*

*I OVERCAME by the blood of the lamb (JESUS) and the word of my testimony! Today I am living an abundant life of freedom through the grace of Christ by Faith. He has won the Victory!*

*I OVERCAME by doing the work! I did not give myself a pass to live in pity.*

*The same goes for you!*

Choose to no longer be a victim, but an OVERCOMER!!!!

Tap into your God-given dominion, authority, ability, gifts and talents and began to LET YOU ARISE!!!

# <u>Reflection Journal</u>

Journal your Overcoming process...

_____

_____

_____

_____

_____

_____

_____

_____

_____

_____

_____

_____

_____

_____

_____

_____

# <u>Works Cited</u>

Child Sexual Abuse Statistics,
victimsofcrime.org/media/reporting-on-child-sexual-abuse/
child-sexual-abuse-statisticsinvisiblechidlren.org

"Child Sexual Abuse Statistics." Darkness to Light,
www.d2l.org/the-issue/statistics/.

The Bible - KJV